EARTH
STORY

ERIC MADDERN
illustrations by
LEO DUFF

In the beginning was nothing at all,
only silence, stillness and black.

Then, in the first moment
long, long, long, LONG ago,
out of nothing came something . . .

. . . An enormous bang
and a blinding flash of light!
In one scorching hot moment
everything began.

Who knows how?
Who knows why?

Light streamed everywhere, pushing out darkness all around

then cooling into the first stuff,
hot clouds of gas.
And the hot gas went spinning, swirling,
like giant whirlpools of smoky light,
racing out, out and away,
becoming great galaxies.

Inside one misty galaxy
bright points of light shone out:
like droplets of breath on a cold window pane
the twinkling stars were born.

Some were big and blue and very, very hot
but quickly burned themselves up.
Some were small and red and not very hot
but lasted for ever and ever.
And some of the stars were middling hot,
not so big nor very little.
They lasted for a good long time.
They were the yellow stars.

One yellow star was special.
At first it was just a bulge in the middle
of a whirling saucer of dust.
But as dust and gas swirled inward
the bulge got bigger and bigger.

It began to get tighter and tighter,
and hotter and hotter and hotter,
until at last it was so hot
that it burst into flames,
flashed on its starlight
and became our Sun.

The disc of dust spinning around the sun
split into many rings.
Then each ring slowly squashed to a ball
making a scatter of planets.
The ones near the sun were small and rocky
and hot from being so close.
The faraway planets were gassy and icy
like frozen giants in space.

But the third planet out wasn't freezing or hot,
not huge nor very small.
It was just in the middle, which made it quite special.
It was our planet Earth.

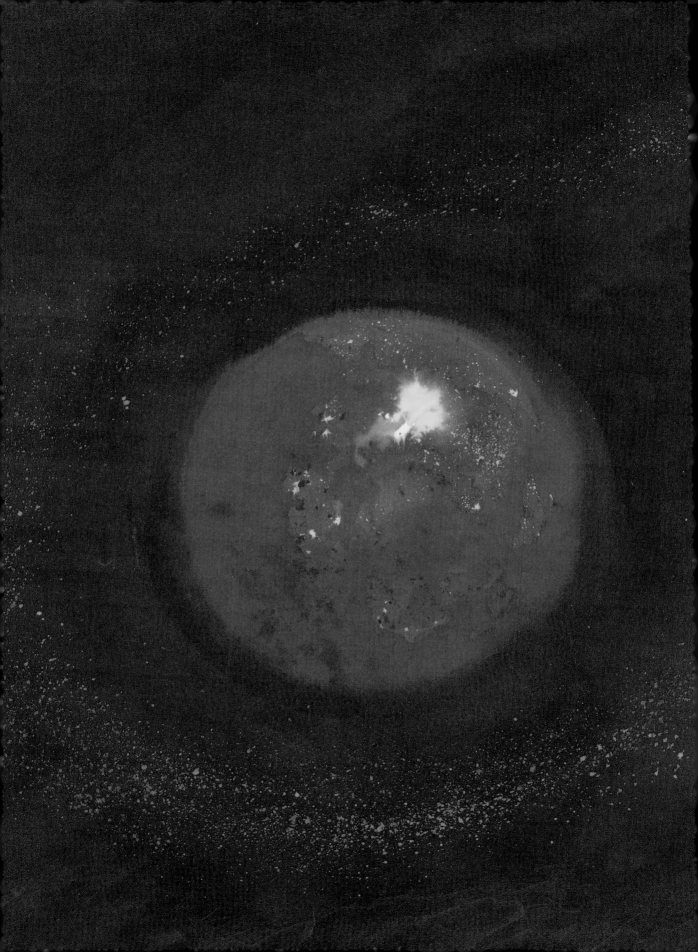

And the Earth was also special
because it wasn't formed alone,
for out of its spinning ring of dust
a smaller rock ball was born.
It circled the Earth like a tiny planet,
taking one month to go round.
Like a constant friend it was always there,
and has been there since,
pushing and pulling, waxing and waning.
It was our Moon.

At first the Earth was very hot
like a bubbling cauldron of melted rock.
But slowly the heavier rocks like iron
sank to the fiery core of the Earth,
and the light rocks floated up to the top,
cooling into a crisp crust.

Between crust and core was a moving layer;
like thick glue it oozed about,
carrying the crust, crinkling and cracking it,
lifting and shifting it, making the ground.

Then from under the ground
through the cracks and the holes
spouted melted rock making great volcanoes.
They rumbled and grumbled;
they growled and they roared
until hot flowing lava poured everywhere.
Breathing fire like dragons, spitting gases and steam,
volcanoes became the first mountains.

Slowly, slowly the Earth cooled down,
the rocks grew hard,
and the steam in the sky
turned to heavy black clouds.
Then at last it began to rain.

It rained and rained for millions of years:
thunder cracking, lightning flashing
torrents of water splashing to the ground,
flowing into rivers and streams,
flooding out to lakes and seas.

Every splash of rain
washed away a speck of rock,
wearing down the jagged peaks,
crumbling them into broken shapes
like boulders and craggy hills.
The rivers carried mud to the valleys and plains,
washed out salt to the sparkling sea
and the crashing waves made sand on the shore.
Then, in the warm ponds and shallow seas,
under the gentle pull of the moon,
something new began to happen,
something special on Earth.

It was very, very small and very, very slow,
but inside the ponds, in every tiny drop,
salt from the rocks, water from the rain,
gas from volcanoes and heat from the sun
began to play with one another . . .
They played for millions of years,
bumping and jumping, whizzing and whirring,
mixing and fixing, holding on and letting go!

Slowly, the tiny bits fitted together
making new squiggly things, just about alive,
that could split in two to make another
little squiggle like themselves.
It was the first life, not much to look at,
but the first life, just right for Earth.

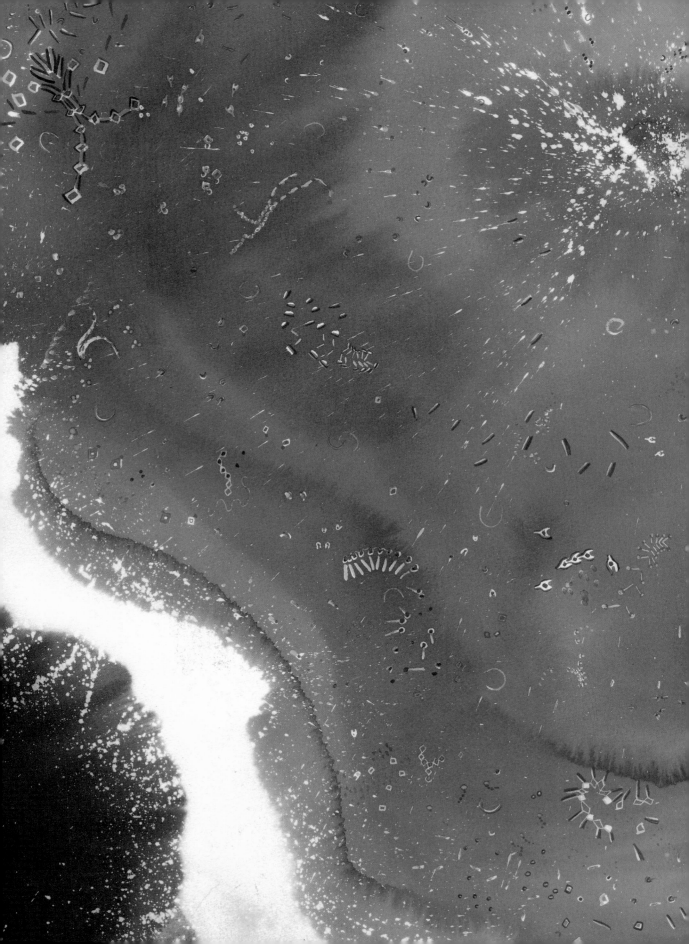

And so it was
that after a long, long time
the Earth was one place
in the great, starry galaxy
ready to come alive.
From its rocky ground and its salty seas,
from its fresh, blowing air, Moon and Sun
came the first living thing:
a clever little squiggle.
And from that, all the life we see today has come,
even you and me!

But that's another story.

First edition for the United States, the Philippines, and
Canada published 1988 by Barron's Educational Series, Inc.

Text © Eric Maddern 1988
Illustrations © Leo Duff 1988

Earth Story was conceived, edited and designed by
Frances Lincoln Limited, Apollo Works,
5 Charlton Kings Road, London, England.

All inquiries should be addressed to:
Barron's Educational Series, Inc.
250 Wireless Boulevard
Hauppauge, New York 11788

International Standard Book No. 0-8120-5909-3

Library of Congress Catalog Card No. 87-73252

Printed and bound in Hong Kong

Design and art direction Debbie MacKinnon
Editor Kathy Henderson